Introduction

This volume, the twelfth of our Collection Series, has been compiled to offer our readers quiet moments in the midst of everyday problems and concerns.

The selections contained in this book were not made because of literary prominence, but to convey messages of hope and peace, which are so beautifully expressed by the poets.

Because of the varied styles and contents of the verses, we feel that each of our readers will find their own favorite pieces in this collection.

Again, we offer our special thanks to our contributing authors and to the publishers for allowing us to include their work in this anthology.

ACKNOWLEDGEMENT: "The Beauty of Jesus" by Alice Hansche Mortenson from LINES TO LIVE BY compiled and edited by Clinton T. Howell by permission of Peggy H. Howell.

Salesian Missions wishes to thank those who have given their kind permission to reprint material included in this book. Every effort has been made to give proper acknowledgements. Any omissions or errors are deeply regretted, and the publisher, upon notification, will be pleased to make necessary corrections in subsequent editions.

Quiet Moments

from the
Salesian Collection

Compiled and Edited
by Sara Tarascio

Illustrated by
Paul Scully
Frank Massa
and
Russell Bushée

CONTENTS

My Own Backyard

Dear Lord, when things get hectic,
And living seems so hard,
I just go out and sit awhile,
Within my own backyard.
For there it's quiet and peaceful,
Beneath the shady trees,
And sunlight through the branches,
Accompanies every breeze.

There are a dozen shades of green,
Designed to please the eye,
Chubby squirrels and humming birds,
. . . A golden butterfly.
The honeysuckle's perfume,
Permeates the air,
And though I do not see Him,
I know that God is here.

The sky so high above my head,
Is an electric blue,
And there are lazy cotton clouds,
With nothing else to do,
But sail across the heavens,
And yet I know that I
Was given hope whose sturdy wings
Were also meant to fly.

This old world we inhabit,
Is much the worse for wear,
Beauty fades so quickly,
And hearts forget to care.
But somehow I've discovered,
Within my own backyard,
A peaceful sanctuary,
. . . In which I find the Lord.

Grace E. Easley

7

Ideals Are Like Stars

In this world of casual carelessness
    it's discouraging to try
To keep our morals and standards
    and our ideals high . . .
We are ridiculed and laughed at
    by the smart sophisticate
Who proclaims in brittle banter
    that such things are out of date . . .
But no life is worth the living
    unless it's built on truth,
And we lay our life's foundation
    in the golden years of youth . . .
So allow no one to stop you
    or hinder you from laying
A firm and strong foundation
    made of faith and love and praying . . .

And remember that ideals
   are like stars up in the sky,
You can never really reach them,
   hanging in the heavens high . . .
But like the mighty mariner
   who sailed the storm-tossed sea,
And used the stars to chart his course
   with skill and certainty,
You too can chart your course in life
   with high ideals and love,
For high ideals are like the stars
   that light the sky above . . .
You cannot ever reach them,
   but lift your heart up high
And your life will be as shining
   as the stars up in the sky.

Helen Steiner Rice

Used with permission of
The Helen Steiner Rice Foundation
Suite 2100 Atrium Two
221 E. Fourth Street
Cincinnati, OH 45202

The Disappointed

There are songs enough for the hero
   Who dwells on the heights of fame;
I sing of the disappointed —
   For those who have missed their aim.

I sing for the breathless runner,
   The eager, anxious soul,
Who falls with his strength exhausted,
   Almost in sight of the goal;

For the hearts that break in silence,
   With a sorrow all unknown,
For those who need companions,
   Yet walk their ways alone.

There are songs enough for the lovers
   Who share love's tender pain,
I sing for the one whose passion
   Is given all in vain.

And I know the solar system
   Must somewhere keep in space
A prize for that spent runner
   Who barely lost the race.

For the plan would be imperfect
   Unless it held some sphere
That paid for the toil and talent
   And love that are wasted here.

Ella Wheeler Wilcox

God Is Never Far Away

God is never far away.
I can see Him every day:

In the caring things you do,
I can see God's love — in you;
In the gentle words you say,
I can see His gentle way;
In your touch, I feel Him near;
In your smile, I hold Him dear;
In our children's songs and cries,
I can hear His loving sighs.
By the forest, lake and stream,
I can see His gift of dreams;
By the ocean's rhythmic roar,
I hear music He has scored;
And — in nature's varied sights,
I can see His strength and might
That remind me — with enthrall —
He is Master, over all.

God is never far away.
I can see Him every day.

Michael Dubina

Teach Me, Lord

Oh teach me, Lord, to treasure much
The simple things of life — the touch
Of wind and snow, of rain and sun;
And when the hours of work are done,
The quietness of rest, the fair
And healing sustenance of prayer.
And, Lord of living, help me keep
A shining, singing gladness deep
Within for blessings yet to be
Through all eternity.

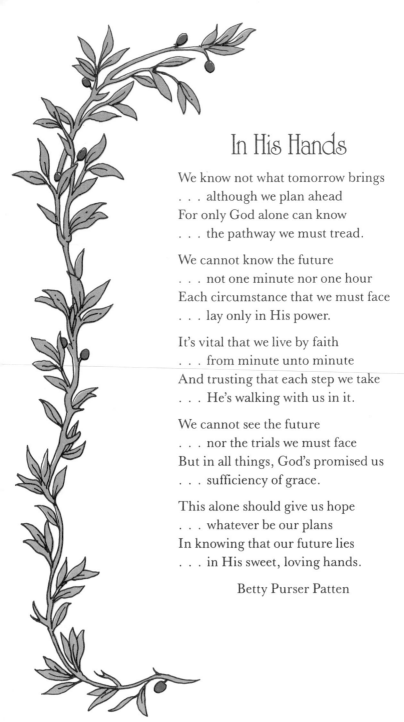

In His Hands

We know not what tomorrow brings
. . . although we plan ahead
For only God alone can know
. . . the pathway we must tread.

We cannot know the future
. . . not one minute nor one hour
Each circumstance that we must face
. . . lay only in His power.

It's vital that we live by faith
. . . from minute unto minute
And trusting that each step we take
. . . He's walking with us in it.

We cannot see the future
. . . nor the trials we must face
But in all things, God's promised us
. . . sufficiency of grace.

This alone should give us hope
. . . whatever be our plans
In knowing that our future lies
. . . in His sweet, loving hands.

Betty Purser Patten

It Doesn't Matter

It doesn't matter who you are,
Or what you want to be;
What matters is what's in your heart
That helps to make you free . . .

It doesn't matter who you are,
Or where you want to go;
What matters is Who guides your steps
Because He loves you so . . .

It doesn't matter who you are,
Or how much you can give;
What matters is what's in your soul,
And how you choose to live . . .

It doesn't matter who you are,
Or what you want to do;
What matters is your faith in God
That makes you pure and new . . .

It doesn't matter who you are,
Or what you have to share;
What matters is that you believe,
And call on God in prayer!

Hope C. Oberhelman

Thank You, Lord

Thank You, Lord, for knowing me
As no one has before,
For all Your gifts, and even when
I sometimes ask for more.
Thank You, Lord, for standing by
Though times be good or bad,
For never throwing up to me,
The chances I have had.

Thank You, Lord, for picking up
The pieces when they fall,
For always being near enough
To hear me when I call.
Thank You, Lord, for holding on
To me when I would go,
For finding deep within my soul,
The things that never show.

Thank You, Lord, for promises
You never fail to keep,
For counting every heartbeat
When I lay me down to sleep.
Thank You, Lord, for mercy
And for wisdom that You show,
For sometimes saying "Yes" to me,
. . . And sometimes saying "No".

Thank You, Lord, for patience
When I feel like giving up,
For adding honey to the dregs
I taste within my cup.
Thank You, Lord, for loving me
As no one ever can,
For wishing me an Angel,
But for seeing me . . . a man.

Grace E. Easley

My Day

The potted plant on the windowsill,
The half-cooked roast in the oven,
The distant call of a whippoorwill,
All are things I'm lovin'!
As is the green lawn near my door,
The sun on the old brick street,
The leisurely stroll to the corner store,
The good neighbors that I meet.
I love life at a not too frantic pace,
Savoring delights on my way,
As the moon caresses earth's moody face,
I give thanks to God for my day.

Dorothy Niederberger

Try

Set your sights above your head
And always keep them high.
And don't allow it to be said
You ever failed to try.

For trying is the all of life
And if you struggle so
That you are always in the strife,
You'll high and higher go.

And as you face life's rugged hill,
Keep climbing for the top.
And if you never reach it, still,
You can't be called a flop.

Yes, always try to do your best
And don't sit down crying.
No one can say he's no success
Who goes through life, trying.

Wesley Yonts

Rosebud Prayers

Prayers are like rosebuds . . .
That are not as yet in bloom . . .
But if you'll just keep on believing . . .
They'll release their fragrance soon . . .

For each prayer like a petal . . .
Will unfold in its time . . .
And when they all have opened . . .
Then the outcome is divine . . .

For God in all His glory . . .
Will not fail us in His task . . .
For He views us as a "rosebud" . . .
but He does want us to ask . . .

Chris Zambernard

Your Gospel

There's a sweet old story translated for us,
    which was written, long ago,
The gospel according to Mark, Luke, and John,
    Of Christ and His mission below.

We read and admire the gospel of Christ,
    With its love so unfailing and true —
But what do they say and what do they think
    Of the "gospel according to you"?

It's a wonderful story, that gospel of love,
    As it shines in the Christ-life divine,
And oh that its truth might be told once again
    In the story of your life and mine.

Unselfishness mirrors in every scene,
    Love blossoms on every sod,
And back from its vision the heart comes to tell
    The wonderful goodness of God.

You are writing each day a letter to all,
    So take care that the writing is true . . .
It's the only gospel that some will read;
    That "gospel according to you."

Amazing Grace

The shadows may be dark and deep,
　　and night so still you cannot sleep,
and all the friends you love are gone,
　　and passing time may drag till dawn;
Your mind may dwell on past harms done
　　(like clouds, such thoughts hide light of sun)
and money-worries be like weeds
　　that choke the growth of better seeds.
Lost hopes and dreams for better things
　　may make ears deaf to bird that sings
of living fully in the now —
　　not nursing cares that crease your brow.

Storms may sweep on us much too fast
    to close a window till they're past —
yet, though the rain pools on the floor,
    we still rush to look out the door
rejoicing at a rainbow bright
    with special promise in its light.
When we see only hate and strife,
    our anger's passion cripples life.
But agony is sure to go
    when we can trust the love we know.
Our strength comes in the faith to hear,
    "Fear not, my child, for I am near."

                    Eugene G.E. Botelho

Thy Power

Father, do Thou this day free me . . .

From fear of the future,
From anxiety for tomorrow,
From bitterness toward anyone,
From cowardice in face of danger,
From laziness in face of work,
From failure before opportunity,
From weakness when Thy power is at hand.

But fill me, I beseech Thee, with . . .

Love that knows no barriers,
Courage that cannot be shaken,
Faith strong enough for the darkness,
Strength sufficient for my tasks,
Loyalty to Thy kingdom's goal,
Wisdom to meet life's complexities,
Grace to meet life's perplexities,
Power to lift others unto Thee.

Blessings Every Day

The view seen from my window
   Would any heart delight,
As luscious hills and valleys
   Provide a stunning sight.

The murmur of soft breezes,
   The warbling of the birds,
The patter of the raindrops,
   Make the sweetest music heard.

The scent of honeysuckle,
   Lilac, rose and pine,
Can titillate my senses
   And create a joy sublime.

I walk in dew-kissed meadows
   And feel the morning sun,
And twinkling stars and moonlight
   Appear when day is done.

I taste the varied pleasures
   Of life's miracles each day,
And count the many blessings
   That the Lord has sent my way.

       Catherine Janssen Irwin

Cast Your Bread

Cast your bread
upon the waters
and it comes floating
back to thee.

'Tis true of every
word and deed we cast
upon life's sea.

Diane Denise Lake

This Day

Yesterday is gone now,
Tomorrow is yet to be, —
I must live my life,
In this day's reality.

I'll not spend my time,
Thinking of the past,
Or planning for the future,
This day, I'm free, at last!

I'll forgive myself,
For errors I have done,
I'll keep my planning flexible, —
For each new day to come!

This day I'm not the same,
A new and different me,
Gives thanks for joy and promise,
For blessings yet to be!

New vision floods my mind,
Fresh opportunities,
New chances for fulfillment,
Great possibilities!

I'll make each moment count,
I'll try to do and say,
The things that give life meaning,
I may only have THIS DAY!

Micky Meyer Mathewson

Trust

When all seems lost, and the future dim,
The Lord will help, just turn to Him;
When dreams are gone, and you can't cope,
God's endless love will give you hope.
He knows your needs, He'll show the way
To meet your problems day by day;
His strength and help will be with you,
Just let Him in, His light shine through.
Trust in God, He's always there
To hold you in His loving care.

Ruth Moyer Gilmour

Faith

Faith is holding on to life,
When all around is pain;
Faith is seeing rainbows
When the sky is full of rain . . .

Faith is reaching out to God
When you are filled with fear;
Faith is taking someone's hand,
And feeling God is near . . .

Faith is walking in the dark,
And looking for the light —
Faith is knowing God is love,
And trusting in His might . . .

Faith is showing you believe,
And that you truly care;
Faith is searching for the Lord,
And finding Him in prayer!

Hope C. Oberhelman

Thank You, Lord

Thank you, Lord, for rocking chairs
And parents who have graying hairs,
Thank you for the rainy day
And mud piles where the children play.

Thank you, Lord, for thermometers
And glasses when the vision blurs,
Thanks for pews with padded seats
And socks that are darned and mended sheets.

Thank you, Lord, for swimming holes
And wiggly worms and fishing poles,
And vaporizers in the night
And candles when we have no light.

Thank you for the waving flag
And those who serve when others lag,
Thank you for the beans we string
For crutches and the walking cane.

Thank you, Lord, for ivory flakes
For leaves that fall and tools that rake,
For day old bread and remade stew
For all these things, Lord, we thank you.

Thank you, Lord, for trials we face
And victory gained, by Your grace
And thank you for all battles won
Through Christ, Your dear Beloved Son.

Betty Purser Patten

My Visit with God

I'm here to spend an hour, Lord,
Just visiting with You;
I'd like to tell You all about
The things I want to do.

I want to ask Your loving help
In all the things I've planned;
Unless they are against Your will,
For You are in command.

I'll just sit here for awhile
In silent thought with You;
Your love will soothe my troubled heart
And all my strength renew.

                        Delphine LeDoux

Life's Wonders

I've never touched a rainbow
And yet I see it there,
Within the sky so far away
Its colors soft and fair,
The wind is quite elusive
And yet I feel its breeze,
And watch it touch the treetops
And gently move the leaves.

Our God within the heavens
I cannot see His face,
And still I feel His presence
And know His saving grace,
The wonders of a rosebud
That opens to the sun,
Each miracle of dawning
And stars when day is done.

The glowing far-off sunset
Untouched by human hands,
So much a part of living
A heart still understands,
We needn't see our Saviour
To feel His loving care,
Life's wonders still shall bless us
Each time we kneel in prayer.

Garnett Ann Schultz

Home Is Where the Flowers Bloom

Home is where the flowers bloom
   and children love to play,
And mother's whispered lullaby
   is heard at end of day.

Home is where the Bible's read
   and children learn to pray
Before they hurry off to school
   and put their toys away.

Home is where you live a dream
   that others make come true
Because they love you as you are
   and want the best for you.

Home is where the years fly by
   on wings of solid gold
And mem'ries are precious gems
   to treasure when we're old.

Home is where the flowers bloom
   although we are apart,
And we can smell the roses
   forever in our heart.

Clay Harrison

New Friends and Old Friends

Make new friends, but keep the old;
Those are silver, these are gold.
New-made friendships, like new wine,
Age will mellow and refine.
Friendships that have stood the test,
Time and change — are surely best.
Brow may wrinkle, hair grow gray,
Friendship never knows decay.
For 'mid old friends, tried and true,
Once more we our youth renew.
But old friends, alas! may die,
New friends must their place supply.
Cherish friendship in your breast —
New is good, but old is best,
Make new friends, but keep the old;
Those are silver, these are gold.

Joseph Parry

The Snows Will Come

The snows will come in their time,
   Where all is cold and still,
   Where summer flowers once grew
   And brightened your window sill.

Life's storms will come, friend of mine,
   Where doubt and fear assail,
   Where strong assurance you knew
   Will falter and seem to fail.

But have no fear, gentle heart,
   The fiercest gale must cease
   And in its wake, calm shall come
   And bring you deep faith and peace!

     Kathryn Thorne Bowsher

The Glory of Spring

Lacy leaves of emerald green
Adorn the naked trees,
Now that spring is here again
To beautify the scene.
In many dormant garden beds
New life begins to stir,
Flowers show their pretty heads
Like maidens pure and fair.
Pussy willows seem to purr
In the sunshine's glow
Like baby kittens, in new furs,
Prepared for sudden snow,
That often comes as a surprise
But does not linger long
Underneath the warming skies,
Now that winter's gone.

Elsie Natalie Brady

Be Not Afraid

"Be not afraid" the Master said,
"I'm with you always," so instead
Of shouldering my cross alone,
I place my burden on His own.
For I'm not nearly strong enough,
To make it when the going's rough,
And it's a comfort to believe
"You need but ask Me to receive".

Handed down to me through time,
These blessed words of hope, and I'm
Renewed in spirit to recall
"Am I not Father to you all"?
One day these feet shall cease to roam,
Earth's but my temporary home . . .
I was in truth for Heaven made,
And so I shall not be afraid.

Grace E. Easley

Sail On

Life, a searching sailing ship,
   takes us on an endless trip
      to seek the harbor of peace
         by the shore where heartaches cease.

Faith, the sail to check our doubt,
   catches the wind as we come about.
Hope, the line that trims our sail,
   evens the shifts of calm or gale.
Love, the rudder to guide our course,
   channels the grace to the living Source.

Life, an ageless sailing ship,
   takes us on a timeless trip
      to find the port where we can rest
         at last, home in His caress.

Janet Collins

Do Not Despair

Do not despair,
Let not dismay
Impair your vision
For today . . .
Though sunny skies
Have disappeared,
While thunder sounds
And storm-cloud nears;
Do not lose hope
For He abides . . .
A Faithful Friend,
Close at your side.

Anna Lee Edwards McAlpin

In Heaven We'll Understand

Not now, but in the coming years
    It may be in the Heavenly Land,
We'll read the meaning of our tears;
    Some day, in Heaven we'll understand.

We'll know why clouds instead of sun
    Were over many a cherished plan;
Why smiles have ceased when just begun;
    Some day, in Heaven we'll understand.

Then trust in God, through all thy days
    Fear not for He doth hold thy hand;
But, whilst you live, still sing and praise;
    Some day, in Heaven we'll understand.

Thanksgiving

Oh precious Father, as we bow
  Before Thy throne today,
We count the many blessings
  Thou hast showered upon our way.

The comfort of our humble homes
  Our health and happiness,
The strength provided for each day
  To meet the strain and stress.

We thank Thee for Thy precious Son
  Who brought salvation free,
And for this mighty land of ours,
  A land of liberty!

So, Lord, help us to give Thee thanks
  For all that we hold dear,
Not only on Thanksgiving Day
  But each day of the year.

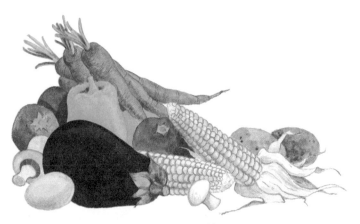

God's Blessings

I thank God for the blessings
That He bestows on me,
I know I am not worthy
And cannot hope to be.

He always has inclined His ear
When I seek Him in prayer,
And when I need a helping hand
I always find Him there.

I kneel to Him each new born morn
And, too, at close of day,
And offer my most grateful thanks
In my own humble way.

Without His countless blessings
So void my life would be.
He has enriched it every way
By blessings given me.

                   Harold F. Mohn

It Only Takes a Moment

A simple act of kindness,
A bit of love to spare
Can make a world of difference
Between hope and despair.

It only takes a moment
To stop and say hello
To one distraught and lonely
To leave a cheerful glow.

A flower or a handshake
Can brighten up the day
When the friends are gone and loved ones
Are many miles away.

So why not take a moment
To chase away the blues
By making someone happy
To make you happy too.

Elsie Natalie Brady

The Things We Take for Granted

The things we take for granted
 would fill a lengthy book . . .
A sunset by the seashore,
 the babble of a brook.
Red roses in a garden,
 sunflowers growing tall . . .
The majesty of autumn
 when leaves begin to fall.
The budding trees of springtime
 when blue skies follow gray . . .
The lullaby of song birds
 that welcomes every day.
The miracle of childbirth,
 a mother's whispered prayer . . .
The things we take for granted
 prove that God is there!

Clay Harrison

Understanding

The troubles that beset you
   Along life's winding road
Are sent to make you stronger
   To share another's load.

We cannot share a sorrow
   If we haven't grieved a while,
Nor can we feel another's joy
   Until we've learned to smile!

Sweet mystery of music,
   Great masters and their art,
How well we understand them
   When we've known a broken heart!

Let tyrants lust for power,
   Sophisticates be wise,
Just let me see the world, dear God,
   Through understanding eyes.

           Nick Kenny

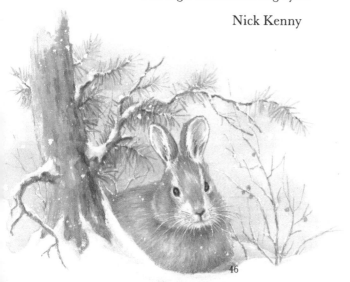

The Little Things

It's the little things in life that count,
　　The things of every day;
Just the simple things that we can do,
　　The kind words we can say.

The little things like a friendly smile
　　For those who may be sad,
The clasp of a hand or kindly deed
　　To help make someone glad.

A knock on the door of lonely homes,
　　Or flowers bright and gay
For someone to whom you might bring cheer
　　With just a small bouquet.

Just the little greetings here and there
　　On which so much depends,
The little pleasures that all can share,
　　The joy of making friends.

　　　　　　　Virginia Katherine Oliver

Wings of the Morning

When unsolved quandries fill my mind
and worrisome problems dangle on the line
  of thought,
to God, I closely cling — not as one
  alone, distraught;
but as woman, whom God has strengthened
through a deepening sense of confidence,
  and lengthened
reliance in Him; knowing, all I fear
  will disappear . . .
Even as the morning breaks across the sky,
bringing light in on its silent wings,
  to live or die.

Roxie Lusk Smith

The Hand of God

I wandered, silent and alone,
Along the dusty road,
When in the quiet of the night,
He helped me lift my load . . .

I wandered, silent and alone,
My heart all full of pain,
When He sent down a ray of sun
To chase away the rain . . .

I wandered, silent and alone,
With sadness in my soul,
When He revealed to me the way
To help me reach my goal . . .

I wandered, silent and alone,
Yet, no matter where I trod,
Along each path and through each lane,
I felt the hand of God!

Hope C. Oberhelman

Trust God

Remember the sun won't always shine
There'll be thunder clouds and rain;
Dreary days and stormy skies
Vicissitudes and pain.

And when your problems mount and grow,
And you can see no end;
Turn to God and trust Him,
He will be your friend.

Talk to God, He'll listen,
When your future looks so dim;
The sun will shine again for you,
When you put your trust in Him.

Ruth Moyer Gilmour

Acceptance

I know the Lord giveth,
And taketh away,
His will must be done,
There's no other way.
But sometimes it seems,
The harder I try,
We both cannot seem
To see eye to eye.

I pray to be humble,
Accept what God sends,
In this way I know
I am making amends,
For times I have hurt Him,
And many they be,
For He never sends crosses,
. . . Too heavy for me.

Grace E. Easley

You're a Winner

You were born to be a winner,
　　There's no way that you can lose,
You just hang in there and whistle,
　　When you're bothered by the blues.

When a best friend disappoints you,
　　And you're crying deep inside,
You just somehow grin and bear it,
　　And your heartaches always hide.

You don't run to catch a rainbow,
　　But the pot of gold you find,
When you stop to smell the roses,
　　You're a winner, every time!

Julie E. Jones

Hold Me, God

Grab me by the shirt tail, God,
If I should start to wander
Hold me with Your patient love
That I'll not look off yonder.

Wrap peace around my days, God,
Let heart-songs rise from within.
Keep me close within Your reach
That I'll not look toward sin.

God, give me comfort in the night
Where dreams come softly sweet.
Wake me to the dawn of morrow
And guide my wayward feet.

Rosa Nelle Anderson

There's Hope in Each New Day

When life is filled with challenges
    Fight back with heart and soul,
Face each one with confidence
    To win your utmost goal.

Anyone can be a winner
    When God is on their side,
Just trust His loving providence
    For it can turn the tide.

And if it is a miracle
    You need to see you through,
You may just find that miracle
    Will wing its way to you.

Catherine Janssen Irwin

Reaching Out

When shadows fall and night descends
I think about this day —
What have I done to help lost souls
That may have passed my way?

Have I reached out to all in need
With gentleness and prayer —
To show them I'm a child of God
And that He really cares?

Each day dear Lord, I live for You
And do the best I can —
For those I've missed, I pray that they
Will pass my way again.

And now I lay me down to sleep
And pray before I wake
For wisdom to reach out once more
When tomorrow's light will break.

Albert Norman Theel

A Blessing

Oh, let me bless in some kind way
　　Each person I will meet today,
For any life that enters mine
　　May love and grace be there to find.

For just a quick and twinkling smile
　　Will lift the heart a little while,
A thoughtful act, a warm embrace
　　Can brighten up the saddest place.

Sweet words of love can bring relief
　　To any heart consumed in grief,
An outstretched hand's a blessed sight
　　A star of hope in darkest night.

Sometimes a word, sometimes a deed
　　Is asked to help a man in need,
For if the cost be great or small,
　　That other life is worth it all!

　　　　　　Kate Watkins Furman

Teach Me

Lord, teach Thy grace, that I may be
A gentle follower of Thee;
That love divine will be the way
I seek to follow every day.

Lord, teach me peace, in every test;
Thy mercy keep me in Thy rest,
Oh, may I in Thy love abound,
Thy works and wonders to expound.

Teach me compassion's tender power
That sheds its glow in darkest hour;
That doth reveal Your purity,
Lighting my path to liberty.

It's not by strength nor by my might,
But by Thy spirit that I fight,
Knowing the joy of sweet release
As I live in Thy grace and peace.

Anna Lee Edwards McAlpin

Holy Guidance

Let me walk with you, Lord Jesus,
  Over all life's beaten trails;
Guide me through life's shades and shadows
  Over paths of least travail;
Lead me by life's great temptations
  To Your Kingdom, up above;
Lead the way, for me to follow,
  To Your world of peace and love.

Do not leave me if I stumble
　　Or my steps begin to slow
For — without Your love to guide me —
　　I will have no place to go.
Let me follow, in Your footsteps,
　　To the path that leads above
And, forever, know Your blessings
　　Of eternal life and love.

　　　　　Michael Dubina

One Tranquil Hour in Church

An hour of repose in a mad, busy week;
A place to reflect — and where better to seek
The answer to problems, unsolved and complex
Problems that threaten to sicken and vex.

One tranquil hour of deep meditation —
Renewal of strength through Christ's revelation.
I need this one hour in God's holy place
For faith and for courage life's trials to face.

Pearl E. Auer

Comfort of Jesus

Whenever I'm weak and weary,
    Lost in deep despair,
It's then I kneel at Jesus' feet
    And I find comfort there.

I tell Him all my troubles
    And ask Him for His care.
He lays His hand upon me
    And I find comfort there.

Whenever you're deep in sorrow
    And don't know what to do,
Kneel at the feet of Jesus,
    And you'll find comfort too.

Tell Him how you're troubled
    And need courage to get through
He'll lay His hand upon you
    And you'll find comfort too.

Then go and tell another
    Who is lost in deep despair
Tell them, oh please tell them
    Of the comfort they can share.

When we kneel at the feet of Jesus
    And let Him our burden bear,
He'll lay His hand upon us
    As we find comfort there.

Gladys Adkins

Though he fall, he will not be utterly cast down
for the Lord upholdeth him with His hand.
    (Ps. 37:24)

A Letter

A letter is the warmest way
To bid a friend the time of day,
A keep-in-touch that brings the smiles,
Across the very longest miles.
And what a wealth of strength and hope,
Is tucked inside an envelope,
Reminding loved ones that you are,
At least in heart, not very far.

In no country, state or camp,
The wealth beneath a postage stamp,
For memories that never age,
Are written down upon each page.
And though it's nice to telephone,
One of the sweetest pleasures known,
Are moments shared in thoughts we send,
. . . That can be read, and read again.

Grace E. Easley

Blessings

Picture just a friendly smile —
that makes your troubles flee,
Or just a loving, touching hand
that's placed upon your knee.

Listen to a soothing word
from one you know who cares —
Or drink a cup of kindness
offered from a friend who shares.

Hear a lovely melody
that fills your heart with glee,
Behold the sweetness of His love
in everything you see.

And as you grow more sensitive
to all His love and peace,
The fears and sorrows you have known
are surely going to cease.

So praise the Lord in daily praise
for blessings you receive,
Just look to Him in all your needs,
and trust Him and believe.

Betty Purser Patten

Those Who Truly Love

Their eyes overlook much that would hurt,
Their ears listen with empathy.
Their tongues bring encouragement.
Their hands are willing and helpful.
Their minds think with Christ.
Their love is universal.

Sr. Mary Gemma Brunke

Living

To travel on a very weary road,
To stumble 'neath a heavy load,
To rise again and trudge along
And smile and sing a cheery song—
    That's living!

To rise at dawning brave and strong,
To help a weaker one along,
To heal a heart with gladder song—
    That's living!

To meet a stranger on the way,
To shake his hand and pass the day,
To speak a word of kindness, too,
And hide the sorrow deep in you—
    That's living!

To stand for right with courage true,
To show with pride the man in you
To fill your life with noble deeds,
A sacrifice to human needs—
    That's living!

To greet life's end with no disgrace,
To meet your Maker face to face,
To feel, along the path you've trod
That you have known both man and God—
    That's living!

So Sweet

When we come face to face with things
    That seem too hard to bear
It is so sweet to go to God
    And leave our burdens there.

It is so sweet to have God's love
    When day is dark as night
And have His comfort and His grace
    Make heavy burdens light.

In loving arms of divine care
    Life's burdens quickly fade
And we can patiently go on
    In peace so sweet and staid.

Loreta Inman

Faith

Faith can move mountains,
No matter how steep,
And calm the rough waters,
No matter how deep.

Faith can change darkness
To heavenly light,
While leading us tranquilly
Out of the night.

All this I can grant, with
Assurance, you see,
For countless are the mountains
Faith has moved for me.

Laura Baker Haynes

Autumn's Table

Autumn's table now is spread
With manna, beauty too;
Its centerpiece of reds and golds
Is glorious to view.

Autumn's table, which reflects
The blessings thus bestowed,
Is garnished with the love of God
From Whom all blessings flow.

Loise Pinkerton Fritz

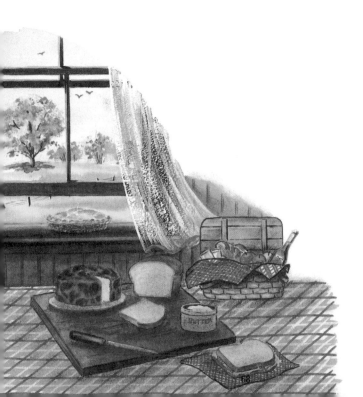

Sonnet in Gold

Warm loaves of golden bread enrich my board,
And marigold lights up a checkered cloth,
Gold honeycomb that droning bees have stored,
And golden cider brimmed with amber froth.
The kitchen curtain unadorned, now yields
Frail beauty lent by golden tints of sun,
And gazing out upon the mellow fields,
I count the golden wheat stacks, freshly done.
A yellow-breasted warbler gaily flits
Where goldenrod extends a lacy span . . .
A brilliant day it is, alive with bits
Of gold the soil relinquishes to man.
In autumn, when the golden leaves are rife,
The child beneath my heart shall come to life!

Esther Nilsson

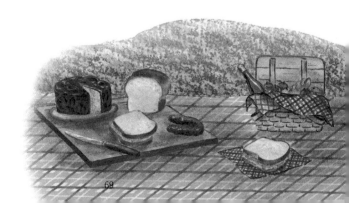

Greet Each Day with Gladness

Greet every day with gladness
   when first you see the light.
There is no need for sadness;
   You made it through the night.

The day may not be perfect;
   The sky may not be blue,
But God will walk beside you
   and help you see it through.

Don't fret about tomorrow,
   Just do your best today
For sunshine follows sorrow
   As blue skies follow gray.

Greet every day with gladness
   As if it were a friend . . .
There may be a blessing waiting
   Somewhere around the bend.

Clay Harrison

— Weeping may endure for a night,
But joy cometh in the morning.

Psalm 30:5

Love: God's Gift Divine

Love is enduring
And patient and kind,
It judges all things
With the heart not the mind,
And love can transform
The most commonplace
Into beauty and splendor
And sweetness and grace . . .
For love is unselfish,
Giving more than it takes,
And no matter what happens
Love never forsakes,
It's faithful and trusting
And always believing,
Guileless and honest
And never deceiving . . .
Yes, love is beyond
What man can define,
For love is immortal
And God's Gift is Divine!

Helen Steiner Rice

Used with permission of
The Helen Steiner Rice Foundation
Suite 2100 Atrium Two
221 E. Fourth St.
Cincinnati, OH 45202

Perseverance

Sail on! weary mariner
Until you reach the heavenly shore
There happiness awaits you
And tribulations are no more.

Dig on, discouraged miner,
Luck may be closer than you think,
The gold that you are seeking
May be in the very next chink.

Reach upward, mountain climber,
For success depends upon you
At the top of the mountain
You'll see a grand, breathtaking view.

Run swiftly, tired athlete,
That you may be given the prize,
It is in perseverance
That the path of victory lies.

    Sr. Mary Gemma Brunke

The Lighthouse of the World

The lighthouse stands on a lonely shore
Shedding a ray in the night;
Ships that are passing keep a close watch
And follow the beam of the light.

God is the lighthouse for all of the world
Shining by day and by night,
Not just a ray to keep you from harm
But a bright eternal light.

For the sailor the light shines just for him
And points the way to the sea;
God's light keeps shining for everyone
And for all eternity.

                    Ruth Moyer Gilmour

*G*od shall be my hope —
my stay, my guide
and lantern
to my feet.

William Shakespeare

He Doeth All Things Well

Our God works in mysterious ways
His wonders to perform.
He's always working for our good
'Tho dark may seem the storm.

Is your life being tossed about?
Trials hard to understand?
God be your anchor. Rest, dear one,
and know He holds your hand.

Have hope! For God will pilot you
And bring you safely through.
Remember behind skies of gray
There shines bright skies of blue.

Have faith! God maketh no mistake
In your life nor in mine;
His perfect wisdom knows what's best
Our beauty to refine.

In His own way and time He'll send
Rich blessings great to tell.
God loves you, friend. Trust Him and know
He doeth all things well.

Beverly J. Anderson

The Master Waits

We worry and we're troubled
    and strive to run our lives;
We're frantic and we're fearful,
    oh, how we agonize —

The sorrow and the misery
    we cause ourselves to bear
When we neglect to go to God
    with everything in prayer —

He knows our every sorrow,
    the burdens that we bear!
We need only take our problems
    and place them in His care!

For all those who are "wearily laden"
    and filled with life's distress
The Master waits to comfort
    and give us peace and rest!

              Elizabeth B. Delea

Remembering to Pray

"Ask and it shall be given",
So the Lord would have you pray.
"Seek and you will surely find",
For He will show the way.
"Knock and it shall be opened",
Do you think God is about
To turn His back upon us,
Knowing all we are without?

We are as little children,
In this valley full of tears,
We need His love to guide us,
And give meaning to the years.
To cross life's troubled waters,
There is not a better way,
Than in clinging to Him tightly,
And remembering to pray.

Grace E. Easley

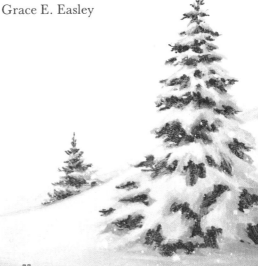

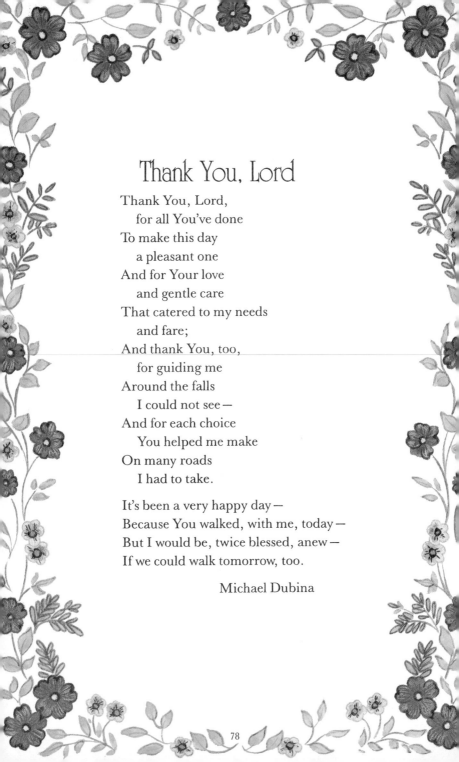

Thank You, Lord

Thank You, Lord,
    for all You've done
To make this day
    a pleasant one
And for Your love
    and gentle care
That catered to my needs
    and fare;
And thank You, too,
    for guiding me
Around the falls
    I could not see —
And for each choice
    You helped me make
On many roads
    I had to take.

It's been a very happy day —
Because You walked, with me, today —
But I would be, twice blessed, anew —
If we could walk tomorrow, too.

                Michael Dubina

Life-Time

Time moves along as must it will
  To make us grow, day older still.
Today is here . . . yesterday gone,
  What's left undone doth linger on.
Time moves along, in yester's 'stead
  A new day dawns to move ahead.
Mistakes were made and this is sure,
  To make amends, endure or cure.

Time moves along, no backward glance,
  With time to come not left to chance.
To fill the dreams that need be filled,
  To till the ground that needs be tilled.
Time moves along, to use or waste,
  The choice to make to suit each taste.
Time to enjoy, to others say,
  "Now is the time to live today".

Time moves along to graying hair,
  To aches and pains and needed care.
Time moves along so very fast
  That most of time of life is past.
Let not sorrow to be our lot,
  It's live today as best we got.
Let not regret of what's been done
  To spoil what's left of time to come.

Robert F. Lowery

I Like Autumn Best

In every season of the year
Rare beauty may be seen,
Bestowed by God in colors fair
    In His creative scheme.
Spring and summer are the times
When flowers are in bloom
With enticing fragrances
    To beautify a room.
There's splendor in a world of white
When gusty north winds blow
And the moon is shining bright
    Upon new fallen snow.
But when the leaves come tumbling down
In gold and crimson dressed,
To lay a carpet on the ground,
    It's autumn I like best.

                Elsie Natalie Brady

God's Colors of Autumn

September is emptying into the Fall
The petals of Summer: The bird's cheery call,
The life-giving sap in the maples and oaks,
The memorable rides on the old country roads.

The picturesque sunsets o'er boat dotted lakes,
The family reunions . . . in groves by the way.
The laughter of children on swings in the park,
The firefly's glow as the evenings grow dark.

September is emptying into the Fall
The petals of Summer (the joys dear to all),
But while Summer's petals are falling from view,
God's colors of Autumn, resplendent, shine through.

Loise Pinkerton Fritz

Don't Give to Me a Present

Don't give to me a present
   with ribbons and a bow,
For if you truly love me
   I would like to know.
Things that mean the most to me
   aren't found within a store,
For it is the little things
   that mean a whole lot more.
A hug or kiss to start the day,
   a smile that says hello
Casts my doubts and fears away
   as love begins to show.
An understanding look will do
   when things are going wrong
To help me sing within my heart
   some old familiar song.
Tender words that show you care
   are precious and so few,
But nothing means as much to me
   as a simple "I love you!"
Don't give to me a present
   with ribbons and a bow,
For if you truly love me
   I really want to know.

          Clay Harrison

Trust and Believe

Whatever our problems, troubles, and sorrows,
If we trust in the Lord,
   there'll be brighter tomorrows,
For there's nothing too much
   for the great God to do,
And all that He asks or expects from you
Is faith that's unshaken
   by tribulations and tears
That keeps growing stronger
   along with the years,
Content in the knowledge that God knows best
And that trouble and sorrow are only a test —
For without God's testing of our soul
It never would reach its ultimate goal . . .
So keep on believing, whatever betide you,
Knowing that God will be with you to guide you,
And all that He promised will be yours to receive
If you trust Him completely and always believe.

Helen Steiner Rice

Used with permission of
The Helen Steiner Rice Foundation
Suite 2100 Atrium Two
221 E. Fourth St.
Cincinnati, OH 45202

A Morning Prayer

Thank you, Lord, for countless things:
Your friendship, mercy, hope in prayer,
For life itself through joy and pain,
The litany each new dawn sings,
Your love like sunshine in the rain.

Thanks for your strength and holy plan
When the way is hard and doubts assail.
Build my resolve in thoughts and deeds
To serve and love my fellowman,
And want no more than daily needs.

Dear Lord, we seek a deeper peace
Than nations show in human kindness.
While there is time, begin the day
When earthly war and strife will cease
And light divine must heal our blindness.

Maurice V. Bochicchio

A Holding Faith

Yesterday, with all its cares,
Its blunders, aches, and sorrow,
Is in the hands of One who holds
The promise of tomorrow.

The sun may rise in roseate clouds,
Or hold a mark of weeping:
The dread of what the day may bring
Is ever in His keeping.

The things that lie within God's will,
A whit is not in changing . . .
No part of hours yet unborn,
Is man's for rearranging.

We blindly add the burdens of
Those two eternities —
The things that were, what is to come —
My times are well with Thee.

Roxie Lusk Smith

"My times are in Thy hand:"
Psalms 31:15

Be Happy Now

Be happy now, rejoice in skies of blue,
Feel the warmth of sun upon your face,
Breathe in the smell of lilacs after rain,
For these are moments you cannot replace.
Pause awhile and listen to the birds,
Within their song so many things you feel.
Watch the glow of fireflies through the dusk,
The moonlight fall across your window sill.

Be happy now, put all your cares aside,
Life is a gift that only God can give,
His dear heart overflows with love for you,
Remember this as long as you shall live.
Let go the tears and grief of yesterday,
Do not destroy the present by the past,
With every dawn a brand new day begins,
. . . Each one a little sweeter than the last!

Grace E. Easley

The Silent Things

It's very strange how silent things
 . . . all sing the Father's praise
The hills and trees, the skies and seas
 . . . shout forth His mighty ways.
A sleeping babe, an empty grave
 . . . are testimonies of
The wonders of a Holy God
 . . . and His unfailing love.
The buds that bloom, the stars and moon
 . . . proclaim His majesty,
The silent things sing praise to God
 . . . in perfect harmony.

Betty Purser Patten

My Daily Creed

Let me be a litle kinder,
　Let me be a little blinder
To the faults of those about me.
　Let me praise a little more,
Let me be, when I am weary,
　Just a little bit more cheery.
Let me serve a little better
　Those that I am striving for.

Let me be a little braver
　When temptations bid me waver,
Let me strive a little harder
　To be all that I should be.
Let me be a little meeker
　With the brother that is weaker,
Let me think more of my neighbor
　And a little less of me.

His Dwelling Place

All His glory and beauty come
    from within,
And there He delights to dwell.
His visits there are frequent,
His conversation sweet,
His comforts refreshing,
    and His peace passing all
    understanding.

Thomas à Kempis

Newness of Life

Spring is the time of newness of life,
A burst of bloom from the earth;
A time of song and hope renewed,
A time that's filled with mirth.
Spring is the time of newness of life
When rejoicing fills the heart,
When all things that seem to lifeless
  be
Are granted a brand new start.

Spring is the time of newness of life,
When old things have passed away:
The winter will all its stormy blasts,
Days tinged with shades of grey.
The time when darkness of winter flees,
As intervenes the light;
Spring represents the newness of life,
Newness of life in Christ.

Loise Pinkerton Fritz

. . . Therefore if any man can be in Christ, he is
a new creature: old things are passed
away; behold, all things are become new . . .
(II Corinthians 5:17)

The world
will never starve
for want of wonders.

Gilbert Keith Chesterton

Awakening

Purple crocuses peeping through the snow,
Bright against their comforter of white,
Heedless of the icy winds that blow,
Spring is on her way and all is right.
Swollen buds upon a blackened branch,
With a touch of crimson showing through,
Flashing wings led home, not just by chance,
Silhouetted there against the blue.

Thawing ice upon a frozen pond,
Tinkles out a frosty crystal tune,
Through the rolling meadows and beyond,
Happy children will be playing soon.
And with all the world brand new again,
Golden gowned forsythia will bloom,
As the morning sun streams softly in
The narrow window of . . . an empty tomb!

Grace E. Easley

The Beauty of Jesus in Me

My life touched yours for a very brief space,
    And what, oh, what did you see?
A hurried, a worried and anxious face,
    Or the beauty of Jesus in me?

Was I steeped so deep in the ways of the
    world
    That you couldn't detect one thing
That would set me apart and show that my
    heart
Belonged to the Heavenly King?

Did I carry no banner for Jesus my Lord,
    Not one thing at all that could show
Whose side I am on in this glorious fight?
    I am His! But you wouldn't know.

Forgive me! And if we should e'er meet again
    Upon earth, oh, I pray you will see
No mark of this world, but His banner
    unfurled,
    And the beauty of Jesus in me!

          Alice Hansche Mortenson

God's Plan

The skies are overcast, and gray
It's just a dreary winter day;
But we should try to understand,
That this is part of God's great plan.

We need some trials here in this life;
Some anxious minutes, and some strife,
So when the peaceful moments come,
We can enjoy our blessings some.

We must have nights along the way,
To make us learn to love the day;
And if the rain would never fall
We'd not enjoy the sun at all.

The wintry winds they need to blow,
And we need sleet, and we need snow;
There is no other way that spring,
Could all its joy and gladness bring.

Wesley Yonts

Rest

Are you very weary? Rest a little bit.
In some quiet corner, fold your hands
  and sit.
Do not let the trials that have grieved
  you all the day
Haunt this quiet corner; drive them
  all away!
Let your heart grow empty of every
  thought unkind
That peace may hover round you, and
  joy may fill your mind.
Count up all your blessings, I'm sure
  they are not few,
That the dear Lord daily just bestows
  on you.
Soon you'll feel so rested, glad you
  stopped a bit,
In this quiet corner, to fold your
  hands and sit.

Climb 'Til Your Dream Comes True

Often your tasks will be many,
And more than you think you can do . . .
Often the road will be rugged
And the hills insurmountable, too . . .
But always remember, the hills ahead
Are never as steep as they seem,
And with Faith in your heart start upward
And climb 'til you reach your dream,
For nothing in life that is worthy
Is ever too hard to achieve
If you have the courage to try it
And you have the Faith to believe . . .
For Faith is a force that is greater
Than knowledge or power or skill
And many defeats turn to triumph
If you trust in God's wisdom and will . . .
For Faith is a mover of mountains,
There's nothing that God cannot do,
So start out today with Faith in your heart
And "Climb 'Til Your Dreams Come True"!

Helen Steiner Rice

. . . If thou canst believe,
all things are possible to him that believeth.
Mark 9:23

The Church

Beautiful is the large church,
With stately arch and steeple;
Neighborly is the small church,
With groups of friendly people;
Reverent is the old church,
With centuries of grace;
And a wooden church or a stone church
Can hold an altar place.
And whether it be a rich church
Or a poor church anywhere,
Truly it is a great church
If God is worshiped there.

Time Limits

If I could live a thousand years
With no disruption of life's span,
There'd be so many special things
I then could do and dream and plan.

A thousand years of life's delights!
Why I could have the longest fling,
And still find ample time to change
Before a final reckoning.

Yet I would also have to bear
As many years of pain and grief,
'Tis best instead the Lord designed
Our time on earth unsure and brief.

Amy C. Ellis

In a Garden

I walked alone in a garden
When the dew was on the ground,
And I felt God's love abiding
In the rich beauty all around;
Dewdrops shone like diamonds
On pansies' velvet dress;
A scarlet rose unfolded
'Neath the sun's caress;
Sweet williams nodded greeting,
Shy violets nestled by,
A meadowlark sang sweetly
'Neath an azure sky.

I thought of a lovely Garden,
Far beyond this vale of tears,
Where God's grace abides forever,
Where there's no night, nor pain,
    nor fears;

Jesus, Rose of Sharon,
Bright shining as the sun,
Sweet lily of the valley,
Fairer than the moon,
Gives life and peace and pardon
From His royal Throne on high,
In Heaven's wondrous Garden—
Haven in the sky.

Kathryn Thorne Bowsher

The Builder

Let me be a builder, Lord,
And with each little nail,
Help me construct a temple
Where all noble things prevail.
And forming its foundation
From the blessed faith of old,
Erect the walls of kindness,
That are lovely to behold.

Let me be a builder, Lord,
Designing all with care,
Raising sturdy beams of hope,
High up into the air.
And with a roof of patience,
And columns made of love,
My edifice should surely please
All heaven up above.

Let me be a builder, Lord,
And may each humble prayer
Be used to strengthen every step
That forms the winding stair.
And thus adhering to the code
All builders must employ,
Become a temple for the soul,
That man cannot destroy.

Grace E. Easley

Risk Love

Fear not to love—
    be swift to care;
    the risk is great,
    your strength is prayer.

Let Jesus' cross
    enflame your soul—
    lay down your life,
    make love your goal.

David L. Hatton

Never Too Late

It's never too late:
   To better try
   Or make amends
   For sins gone by;
      Or better sow
      What love will grow;
      Or better choose
      Which seeds to sow.

It's never too late:
   To better care
   Or better live;
   Or better share;
      Or better give
      Of heart and self—
      And Christian kindness,
      Faith and wealth.

It's never too late:
   To mend your ways
   Or offer "Thanks"—
   For "Thanks", delayed;
      Or better love
      A loving Lord
      Who 'waits your soul,
      With just reward.

It's never too late—
Until you die:
   To better do
   And better try.

          Michael Dubina

I am Always Thine

I will not fear the future
   Nor what's in store for me,
God's love will lead and guide me
   Through all eternity.

His love is ever constant
   And He takes care of me,
He fills my life with blessings
   No harm can come to me.

With faith and hope deep in my heart
   Then peace and joy are mine,
Dear Lord, You're always with me
   And I am always Thine.

Dolores Karides

Stand Firm

My heart is filled with sadness
   For things I see and hear.
I try to live within the now
   And free my mind of fear.

For always in the darkness
   There is a ray of hope,
I'll not give up no matter what,
   My God will help me cope.

So when you feel life's pitfalls
   And all seems so in vain.
Stand firm with Him who loves you —
   You have everything to gain.

Helen Parker

Life Is a Sea

Some days are stormy, some are calm,
   Some days are filled with joy, some strife,
But help me, Lord, that I may be
   Serene upon the sea of life.
Help me to meet whatever comes
   With faith that all is for the best.
If grief be mine, then let me be
   Prepared to pass the acid test.

Life is not difficult when skies
   Are bright and all the sails go well,
But when the clouds are thick and black,
   Yes, that's when character will tell.
For life is like the sea, and storms
   Are bound to happen on the way.
Lord, give me strength and inner faith
   To meet whatever comes my way!

Esther Nilsson

God's Gifts

It isn't only in the towering trees
    nor always in the lovely rose
    that you can find the magic
    in how God's goodness shows.

It does not have to be the wonder
    of an eagle on the wing
    for God has put much beauty
    in many smaller things.

For I see His gift in a butterfly
    and the violet, small and shy,
    and in flowers drinking raindrops
    whenever God's little clouds cry.

Virginia Luers

Never Give Up

They didn't think I could do it
   And said I shouldn't try,
But I kept plodding onward
   Thinking, "Somehow I'll get by."

I admit it hasn't been easy
   And I let things drag a bit,
When I think I can't go on
   I climb on my load and sit.

While sitting there I wonder
   Why it would seem a sin
For me to keep on trying
   And I start plodding on again.

I would give up this minute
   If I thought Jesus didn't care.
But He blesses my every effort
   And helps when I despair.

I'm not striving to win gold medals
   Nor do I covet the victor's cup.
The only thing I ask of Him
   Is the strength to not give up.

If you find your burden heavier
   Than others seem to bear,
Just keep giving it all you've got
   And renew your strength in prayer.

For Jesus is never far away
   From those who call His name.
When we're almost ready to give up
   We're encouraged to try again.

Gladys Adkins

My grace is sufficient for
you, for my power is made perfect in weakness.
(II Cor. 12:9)

When Skies Are Gray

When dark storm clouds obscure the sun
    And hope is looking dim,
Place all your loving trust in God
    And ride the storm with Him.

He never will forsake your trust,
    He's with you for all time,
He'll light the way to rainbowed skies
    And hopes and dreams sublime.

Catherine Janssen Irwin

The Weaver

The weaver takes his canvas
   it is empty and it's bare
And through his eyes of artistry
   he sees a vision there.

He takes his yarn of every hue
   and lays them side by side
And with the magic of his hands
   he weaves a work of pride.

He weaves some sections dark and grey
   and dreary to the eye
And then he'll choose a lovely thread
   made from a golden dye.

And with deftness he will weave
   the threads so there will be
The blending of the different hues
   a lovely tapestry.

He knows the value colors hold
   to form a work of art
So, he weaves gold among the dark
   for balanced counterpart.

And, when the weaver's work is through
   with threads of dark and gold
He has a masterpiece of art
   for mankind to behold.

And so it is in our own lives
   the finished product stands
A masterpiece of priceless worth
   when woven by God's hands.

Betty Purser Patten

You Have a Friend

No matter where your paths may lead,
   no matter what you do,
remember there is one true friend
   who always thinks of you.

Perhaps the roads for you are rough,
   perhaps storms hide the land,
but if you reach out filled with trust
   He'll take you by the hand.

And though you stumble in your fear
   of what Life has in store,
you need not worry — He knows how
   to open Heaven's door.

You cannot leap a thousand miles,
    you'll think each step is slow,
but keep in mind that your good friend
    will help you as you go,

So, take a moment now and then,
    you'll find that He does care . . .
Attune your spirit to His will —
    for love is everywhere.

Wherever you may want to be,
    whatever calls to you,
remember Christ is your best Friend
    and knows what's best for you.

Eugene G.E. Botelho

God's Love

The love of God is infinite,
Encircling all the earth;
Yet it's there for each of us
From the moment of our birth.

It fills each soul with warmth and light;
God's love comes shining through;
Sustaining weary hearts and minds,
And adding strength thereto.

Eternal is God's love for us,
Beginning without end;
He's always known and loved us;
Each one, His special friend.

Delphine LeDoux

Confide in a Friend

When you're tired and worn at the close of day
And things just don't seem to be going your way,
When even your patience has come to an end,
Try taking time out and confide in a friend.

Perhaps he too may have walked the same road
With a much troubled heart and burdensome load,
To find peace and comfort somewhere near the end,
When he stopped long enough to confide in a friend.

For then are most welcome a few words of cheer,
For someone who willingly lends you an ear.
No troubles exist that time cannot mend,
But to get quick relief, just confide in a friend.

Sharing of Blessings

I must share, with you, the blessings
   God has given me this day
And enrich you with the glories
   He has blessed upon my way.
It will join our hearts, together,
   In the loves He made to be
And will multiply the glories
   Of the blessings given me.

I must, also, share the pleasures
   Of my hours of joy and fun
And include you in these blessings,
   By dividing every one,
But it would be more rewarding —
   And a glory, doubly true —
If you, also, shared the blessings
   That the Lord has given you.

Michael Dubina

What We Give, We Gather

The hollow of my heart is small,
A tear can overflow it,
Yet, love can fill its vital parts
And wholly never show it.

You cannot hold it in your hand,
Know whence it comes or goes.
Tears can whelm the smallest heart . . .
From love — it grows and grows.

Buried deep within the soul,
Huge wells of cradled wealth,
For what we give we gather in —
Love multiplies itself.

Just what we feel and what we share,
We keep it not alone.
The greater love we give away
Comes back into our own.

                    Roxie Lusk Smith

Beautiful Spring

O for the beautiful days of spring,
With their soft and gentle breezes,
When winter time is past and gone,
With all the frosts and freezes.

The catalogs of seeds and plants,
The postman now delivers,
And fishermen will soon be seen,
Along the lakes and rivers.

The summertime will soon be here,
And we will hunt for shade,
And now and then we'll hear a wish,
That cooler days had stayed.

Lester E. Bartholomew

I Sat in the Garden

I sat in the garden with God today,
  and with faith I dared to speak.
    I sat beneath a solemn oak,
    close by a gentle creek.

And there we talked of days gone by,
  the good and less than good,
    and in the presence of his peace,
    I clearly understood.

That it mattered not what lay behind,
  or what can be no more;
    but rather what could yet be done
    with the days that lie in store.

For it's not the time that matters most,
  but rather how it's spent
    So I came from the garden renewed,
    for in God my life is content.

Loretta Garing

The Harvest

Who has blessed our golden harvest,
Called the fruits from out the sod,
Made them multiply in number?
Only One: Almighty God.

From the time each seed was planted,
He has watched its nights and days
Till it bore in richest bounty—
So to Him we give the praise.

Marion Schoeberlein

October

Flaming, yellow, crimson dyes —
    Painted on the trees!
Leaflets sighing —
       calling —
       falling —
    Dancing in the breeze!

Night winds sweeping through the sky —
    Melancholy song!
Flowers sighing —
       dreaming —
       dying —
    Drooping in the dawn.

Magic — glory — wonder — beauty!
    Fading into sod!
Autumn praying —
       softly saying,
    "Give them back to God!"

Alice Hansche Mortenson

ever lose an opportunity of seeing
anything that is beautiful,
for beauty is God's handwriting—
a wayside sacrament.
Welcome it in every fair face,
in every fair sky, in every flower,
and thank God for it
as a cup of blessing.

Ralph Waldo Emerson

Spring Tiptoed In

Spring tiptoed softly down the lane
Amidst a gentle April rain,
She touched the earth — each flower bed
And kissed each little tulip head,
Some soft white clouds within the sky
And then a rainbow there on high.

Spring tiptoed down the valley fair
Then up the hillside climbing there,
Across each meadow bright and green
She warmed the little flowing stream,
Then bid the sun to shine so bright
Just at the start of morning's light.

Spring tiptoed in at winter's end
With joys untold she had to lend,
All nature wore a sunny smile
As springtime dressed the world in style,
The blossoms bursting forth in bloom
While nighttime brought a glowing moon.

Across the world she romped in play
Upon this glorious springtime day,
A precious miss with gentle touch
The magic moments loved so much,
A charm where snowflakes once had been
One April day — spring tiptoed in.

Garnett Ann Schultz

October's Glories

October has come with its glories,
A storehouse of treasures to share,
Unmatched is its pageantry's beauty,
No other month can quite compare.

Gone now are the warm days of summer,
Soon winter will pay us a call,
But now we delight in October
The gold interlude in the fall.

Such splendor we'll always remember
Long after the autumn is past;
Preserved in our showcase of memory,
Its glories forever will last.

Beverly J. Anderson

The Autumn Years

Beyond us lie the Autumn years,
Almost before we knew,
An older, somber grey replaced
The younger skies of blue.
God's paintbox over-turned among
The yet uncolored days,
And from the hills and roadsides,
The reds and ambers blaze.

The russet brown of falling leaves,
Sifts down about our feet,
Frost glistens in the sunlight,
The mood is strangely sweet.
Who would have guessed a bird song,
Could move the heart to tears?
Life weaves her richest patterns,
When we reach the Autumn years.

Grace E. Easley

Have Faith

Whene'er you think you stand alone
And all your skies are gray,
Do not lose hope nor heart my friend
Look for a better day.

Do not concede a cause is lost
Though dark it may appear,
For while a spark of life remains
Defeat is never near.

Have faith and seek God's helping hand
To give you strength anew,
And when the clouds have rolled away
You'll find those gray skies blue.

Harold F. Mohn

Give What You Can

It may be just a trifling bit
    That you may have to give,
But give it, for to someone else
    It may mean hope to live!

Give what you can, although it may
    Seem too small to bestow.
No gift is measured by its size,
    How well the needy know!
A wise man said, "The only wealth
    We have is what we share."
Then give. Who knows, your gift may be
    An answer to a prayer!

                    Esther Nilsson

Prayer for Troubled Times

Endow me, Lord, with strength to face
    The bitter trials of life,
Instill within my troubled soul
    Your peace amidst the strife.
Lord, plant a song within my heart
    That I might praise Thee still —
While storms rage on, grant me the faith
    To rest within Your Will.

            Beverly J. Anderson